What are God's plans for you? Jeremiah 29:11

Theresa

Growing Strong in the Storm

Testing Faith and Finding Peace

Theresa A. Salazar

WestBow Press
A DIVISION OF THOMAS NELSON
& ZONDERVAN

Copyright © 2015 Theresa A. Salazar.

All rights reserved. No part of this book may be used or reproduced by any means, graphic, electronic, or mechanical, including photocopying, recording, taping or by any information storage retrieval system without the written permission of the author except in the case of brief quotations embodied in critical articles and reviews.

WestBow Press books may be ordered through booksellers or by contacting:

WestBow Press
A Division of Thomas Nelson & Zondervan
1663 Liberty Drive
Bloomington, IN 47403
www.westbowpress.com
1 (866) 928-1240

Because of the dynamic nature of the Internet, any web addresses or links contained in this book may have changed since publication and may no longer be valid. The views expressed in this work are solely those of the author and do not necessarily reflect the views of the publisher, and the publisher hereby disclaims any responsibility for them.

Any people depicted in stock imagery provided by Thinkstock are models, and such images are being used for illustrative purposes only. Certain stock imagery © Thinkstock.

ISBN: 978-1-5127-0684-0 (sc)
ISBN: 978-1-5127-0685-7 (e)

Library of Congress Control Number: 2015912593

Print information available on the last page.

WestBow Press rev. date: 09/01/2015

Contents

Dedication vii
Preface ix
Acknowledgment xiii
Introduction xv
Prologue xvii

Chapter 1   Stepping Out In The Storm 1
Chapter 2   Preparing For The Storm 9
Chapter 3   Ignoring The Forecast 15
Chapter 4   The Storm Starts To Roll 21
Chapter 5   The Boat Rocks And Changes Course 29
Chapter 6   Running From The Storm 37
Chapter 7   The Storm Arrives 43
Chapter 8   Finding Peace In The Storm 49
Chapter 9   Standing After The Storm 55
Chapter 10 Another Storm, Another Lesson 61
Chapter 11 Building A Shelter From Life's Storms 69

References 79

Dedication

The following pages are dedicated to the man
who promised to stand beside me

"For Better or Worse, Richer or Poorer, In Sickness and Health".

Who knew we'd experience all of these together in one short year?
Roger Salazar, I love you and am blessed to be your wife.

PREFACE

Thank You Is Never Enough

The story you are about to read is a direct result of our obedience to God's instruction to learn and grow. We would never have been ready to weather the storms that were about to crash ashore in our lives without several people that came alongside us and helped us grow. God gets all of the glory but He had several servants who helped to point us to the source of safety.

We were blessed to be part of an intentional discipleship group through our church and would not be where we are today without the people in that group. We are thankful for Bob and Joan who opened up their home and hearts. Andy and Lori were part of the first group and provided great insight and examples of God's love.

Our discipleship group changed over the years and we eventually developed deep loving relationships with a few people. Mark and Donna were our fearless leaders and have been by our side through many of the storms you will read about in the following pages. They guided us and have been excellent examples of God's love over the years.

George and Rosemary are extra special. We were blessed to be included in their very special wedding day and a recent trip to Israel with them. We are so thankful for their honest and pure devotion to each other and their desire to grow in faith.

Mazie joined our group during a transition period and quickly became a solid example of what it means to walk with the Lord. Her ability to make me see the obvious without making me feel blind is a gift from God. She is one of God's special servants and loved by all who know her.

None of this would have been possible without the tremendous teaching and patience of our pastor, Dr. Joe R. Olachea, Jr. and his wife, Kim. We were thrilled to tour the Holy Land with them recently and brought the lessons we've learned from their teaching over the years to life. The Bible will be read in Technicolor from now on because of their dedication to helping all of us grow.

Finally, and most importantly, I must express my extreme gratitude for my loving husband, Roger. He is the greatest gift God has given me and helps me weather life's storms with grace and humility. He has been by my side when times were tough, when the weather was rough, and when others may have turned and left me to battle the storm on my own. I love him beyond words – to the moon and back.

Acknowledgment

I am so thankful and indebted to the help I received from the following people during the creation of this book. I could not have finished this work without the loving feedback and thoughtful insight from Brenda Kammerer, Donna Hull, Wendy Harkness, and Dr. Joe R. Olachea, Jr. They are an inspiration and their help in creating this book was priceless.

Introduction

Have you ever wondered how some people just manage to never have any storms in their lives? Why does it seem like you are always weathering one disaster after another and can never find any peace?

Well, I'm here to tell you we all have storms blow through our lives. The way we handle those storms can make all the difference between living a life of peace or a life spent chasing after fires. You can find peace and comfort no matter what storms blow into your life.

The key to finding the peace we all seek is knowing where to look. Some people are blessed to be born in to a family that teaches them from a young age where to look in times of trouble. Many of us are not so fortunate and spend years trying to control things that are not ours to control. Living a life of peace is not an unattainable goal meant only for the lucky or those unwilling to face reality. Living a life of peace is about knowing God and trusting Him no matter what happens.

Storms will happen in your life. They've happened in ours, and we came through them stronger and more prepared for what may come in the future. We found our life jackets and you can, too.

PROLOGUE

Hurricane Sandy, Superstorm Sandy, "Frankenstorm"

Hurricane Sandy was the deadliest and costliest storm of the 2012 hurricane season. It was the second most costly storm in United States history, second only to Hurricane Katrina. Sandy was responsible for at least 285 deaths along its path of destruction through the Caribbean and the east coast of the United States.

The storm originated in the Caribbean Sea on October 19, 2012 as a tropical wave. It became a Category 1 hurricane on October 23rd and headed for Jamaica. Sandy arrived in Kingston, Jamaica on October 24th with winds of 80 mph. The storm continued to strengthen and struck southeastern Cuba on October 25th as a Category 2 hurricane. It arrived in Haiti the same day and resulted in the deaths of 51 people.

Sandy weakened a bit as it travelled over land on October 26th but that didn't lessen the concern for the United States. Governors up and down the east coast of the United States declared States of Emergency and began to prepare for the storm's arrival. The storm was downgraded to a tropical storm on October 27th and then strengthened back to a Category 1 hurricane by end of day.

New Jersey's governor ordered residents living on the state's barrier islands to evacuate. Amtrak cancelled several of its runs that originated or ended at east coast stations. President Barack Obama declared a State of Emergency for several states on October 28th as airlines began to cancel flights and additional transportation systems began to cancel service.

Hurricane Sandy approached land on Monday, October 29th as a Category 2 storm with hurricane force winds extending 175 miles away from the eye of the storm. Sandy weakened again to a post-tropical cyclone that evening as it made landfall along the coast of New Jersey. The timing of the storm could not have been any worse as it made landfall during a full moon, resulting in high tides 20% larger than normal.

Damage from this storm was widely felt. The outer-bands of Hurricane Sandy resulted in destructive thunderstorms that damaged homes and lives all along the east coast. Massive flooding hit New Jersey, New York and Connecticut. Streets and subway lines were flooded under the enormous amount of water the storm brought with it.

Sandy combined with another system coming across from the western United States and continued up to New England. Power outages were common. Residents could not get gasoline for their vehicles due to lack of power at stations and inability to refill tanks. Businesses, schools, and government offices were closed. National Guard units in several states were activated to help with citizen rescues and storm clean-up.

On November 7th, a nor'easter hit areas already impacted by Sandy. The area would continue to feel the effects of this massive and deadly storm for months, even years, to come but hope was not lost. People from all across the United States came to help in the recovery and rebuilding. Churches and civic groups organized efforts to help with the clean-up. Companies, including mine, volunteered a day of work one year later to show the victims of the storm they were not alone. We are never alone in any storm or the rebuilding afterward.

The story you are about to read is about the impacts a storm had on our family and how God saw us safely through. Just like Hurricane Sandy, the storm was massive and long-lasting. The effects of the storm were felt far and wide in our family and some of the wounds are still open as I write this today.

Healing has happened. Restoration can be found. Hope is not lost as long as we keep our eyes on the One who rescues us from life's storms. God provides us with the safety equipment we need to weather any storm as long as we keep our focus on the One that saves us.

Chapter 1

Stepping Out In The Storm

> ²⁸ And Peter answered Him and said,
> "Lord, if it is You, command me to come to You on the water."
> ²⁹ So He said, "Come."
> And when Peter had come down out of the boat,
> he walked on the water to go to Jesus.
> ³⁰ But when he saw that the wind *was* boisterous,
> he was afraid; and beginning to sink he cried out, saying,
> "Lord, save me!"
> Matthew 14:28-30

Life is filled with trials of various shapes and sizes. I like to refer to them as storms. We are all faced with decisions on how to manage those storms as they come into our lives. Very few of us will be tested the way Peter was tested that night, but we are all challenged to keep our eyes on Jesus when going through trials.

It sounds like a simple and easy thing to do but it is often very hard. Just as athletes must train their bodies to react to the challenges of the sport they practice, we must train our hearts to react when we face the challenges that *will* come up in our lives. We face storms of different sizes every day, but the safety in those storms, no matter the size, is always found in the One who can provide true protection and comfort.

Most of us are familiar with the story of Jesus walking on water, but I find it interesting that only Matthew records Peter's testing during that event. Both Mark 6:45-52 and John 6:16-21 tell the story of a storm that rose up after Jesus instructed His disciples to cross the lake without Him. Matthew tells the same story but also includes the account of Peter's reaction to seeing Jesus walk toward them that fateful night.

According to all three Gospels, Jesus had just fed the multitudes with only five loaves of bread and two fishes. He knew the crowd would recognize the miracle He had just performed. He knew they would want to make Him king, even if by force. Jesus also knew this was not the plan, so He went up to the mountain by Himself.

The disciples got into a boat and set off across the lake.

The Bible tells us that around the fourth watch a strong wind blew up and the waters became treacherous. The disciples were straining against the wind, waves, and storm when they saw Jesus walking toward them. At first they were terrified and thought Jesus was a ghost, but Jesus reassured them and told them not to be afraid.

This is where Matthew includes the story of Peter's test. Depending on which perspective you choose to explore, it may be a recording of Peter testing Jesus or of Jesus testing Peter. Either way, the result was the same: Jesus is Jesus and Peter was not.

You see, Peter calls out to Jesus and asks Jesus to prove Himself to the twelve. Peter asks Jesus to command him to go to his Lord. Jesus' response was short and sweet: "Come."

Peter got out of the boat and started walking toward Jesus. After some steps, Peter looked down, saw the waves, and was afraid. That is when Peter started to sink and called out to Jesus to save him. Jesus reached out and pulled Peter from the water.

There are several points that I find interesting in this story. First of all, what was Peter thinking to test Jesus? Had he not just seen Jesus feed thousands of people with only five loaves of bread and two fish?

Weren't the leftovers greater than the amount they had to begin with? How could he possibly doubt that Jesus was capable of walking to them?

No matter what Peter was thinking, we all know Peter had a tendency to *open mouth, insert foot*. He didn't fail to react in the way we would expect him to react. He called out to Jesus to prove Himself and prove Himself He did. Why do we have the same tendency to doubt the power of our Lord?

Our Father in Heaven and our Lord Jesus Christ have proven themselves over and over in my life, yet I still try to solve problems on my own. Most of us are familiar with the old saying, "When all else fails, pray." Well, I wonder why we wait until everything else has failed before we go to the one source of solutions. Shouldn't we pray first and ask questions later?

Certainly, we are instructed to come to the Father with all of our needs. Philippians 4 is filled with instruction to take our needs to God. We read in Philippians 4:6,

> "Be anxious for nothing, but in everything by prayer and supplication, with thanksgiving, let your requests be made known to God."

We are not to worry about things or events. We are to take them to God and leave them at His feet.

Just to be clear, He doesn't *need* us to tell Him. He already knows what we need. He *wants* us to submit our requests in prayer so we can demonstrate that we trust Him to meet our needs. He wants us to know *we need Him*, not the other way around. Philippians 4:19 also tells us,

> "And my God shall supply all your need according to His riches in glory by Christ Jesus."

The Bible doesn't tell us He will supply *some* of our needs but rather *all* of our needs. All we have to do is ask.

If we are worrying about situations in our lives, it is because we haven't given those situations over to God and trusted that He has a solution. We are missing out on the peace and blessings God wants to give us by fellowshipping with Him. We are robbing ourselves of the opportunity to see and experience God's love and provision.

The second thought that comes to mind with this story is that Peter obeyed the command of Jesus to come to Him. As much as we may blame Peter for being impetuous and having the lack of common sense to stay in the boat, he did dare to step out, and for a moment or two, he walked on water with Jesus. What an awesome image to consider when we think what it must have been like to follow Jesus' command and suspend all concern for safety. What an awesome reward, even if only for a moment.

Matthew isn't specific about how many steps Peter took before he realized he was walking on water. The writer does tell us that Peter did walk on water until he began to look at the waves and consider the wind. He took his eyes off Jesus and, as any other human would do, he began to sink. As much as we'd like to blame Peter for foregoing the rational and safe decision of staying in the boat, we have to commend him for having the courage to obey and step out.

Why would anyone be surprised that Peter took his eyes off Jesus? He was human. He was in awe of what was happening, and he knew he couldn't walk on water any more than you or I can walk on water. That is, we can't walk on water without Jesus!

Peter did what all of us would do in our moment of need. He cried out for Jesus to save him as he started to sink. True to form, Jesus reached out and saved Peter from going under the crushing waves. Matthew 14:31-33 finishes the story:

> "And immediately Jesus stretched out his hand and caught him, and said to him, 'O you of little faith, why did you doubt?' And when they got into the boat, the wind ceased. Then those who were in

the boat came and worshiped Him, saying, 'Truly You are the Son of God."

My husband and I have raised five sons. I can picture the reaction of any of our sons if they had been Peter facing that question. In fact, I believe my reaction would have been something along the lines of: *"Little faith? What about these other guys? None of them had the courage to step out!"* Who would blame him if he did respond in that way? Not I.

Matthew is silent on Peter's reaction, choosing to focus on Jesus saving Peter, the men climbing into the boat, and then Jesus calming the storm.

What were the other disciples thinking as Peter stepped out of the boat? Did any of them try to stop him? Did any of them think that he was making a mistake?

None of them dared to question Jesus! None of them dared to step out of the boat.

Many of us have faced challenges in life, and sometimes the solution God puts before us may not make sense to others. We have to know that God will lead us and show us the way if we trust Him, even if others don't understand. Even though Peter was testing Jesus, he trusted Him. He stepped out of the boat.

What were the disciples thinking when Peter and Jesus got back into the boat? Did they think, *"Wow, that was awesome!"*? They had just witnessed Jesus and Peter walking on water. They worshipped Jesus, but they knew Peter was just a man.

I wonder if they were jealous, even just a little. I wonder if any of them thought wrong of Peter for being so impetuous. I wonder what they thought, but wondering is all I can do because the Bible is silent on their thoughts.

We don't have to guess what Jesus thought because Matthew tells us that Jesus scolded Peter's lack of faith. Peter did trust Jesus enough to get out of the boat and take at least a few steps on the water. Where did Peter fail? He took his eyes off Jesus --- and so do we.

The Bible tells us in several places that we are to call upon the name of the Lord and we will be saved. Acts 2:21 says,

> "And it shall come to pass that whoever calls on the name of the Lord shall be saved."

This is further backed-up in Romans 10:13,

> "For 'whoever calls on the name of the Lord shall be saved.'"

And, just in case you need more information on the topic, let's go back to the book of Joel where it is written in 2:32,

> "And it shall come to pass that whoever calls on the name of the Lord shall be saved. For in Mount Zion and in Jerusalem there shall be deliverance. As the Lord has said, among the remnant whom the Lord calls."

Peter called upon the name of Jesus. Peter was saved. But Peter shouldn't have taken his eyes off Jesus and neither should we.

Yes, it's easier said than done, but we need to keep our eyes open to the One who can save us. The *only* one who can save us is Jesus. We need to trust him with all of our storms.

Let's not be too hard on Peter, though. Even though he tested Jesus, he had enough faith to step out of the boat. Even though he took his eyes off Jesus, he trusted enough to call upon him to be saved. Even though he failed the test, he stayed in the class.

As we explore the different storms that can and do happen in our lives, it's important to remember we may periodically take our eyes off the One who saves us from those storms. Learning to trust in the *one source* of peace in any storm will help us to seek first for His rescue. He is always there and always willing to bring us through life's storms.

CHAPTER 2

Preparing For The Storm

> [105] Your word is a lamp to my feet
> And a light to my path.
> Psalm 119:105

The storms of life come in many shapes, sizes and forms. Some are fast moving, bringing a lot of destruction with them like thunderstorms that pop up during hot summer afternoons. Others take longer to develop and move through at a much slower pace but can be isolating and cold like winter blizzards. All storms have the capability to leave behind years' worth of damage and pain.

We cannot stop the storms from coming, but we can learn better ways to live through them. I pray this story about one particular storm that affected my family in 2012 will help you weather the storms life can bring and find the peace that can only come from the one true source.

My husband and I were married in 2002. Our marriage joined two families of growing young boys. I brought three sons into the marriage and my husband brought two. We stood in the front of my church and recited the standard vows but had no idea how those vows of "for better or for worse, for richer or for poorer, in sickness and in health" would be tested a mere decade later.

To fully understand the impact of the events that happened in our family in 2012, we must start a little further back. Our family, like many families, had been going through a lot of changes through the years. Our sons were growing up, becoming teenagers and adults. Some were moving on to new adventures. A few were presenting challenges along the way. All the while, my husband and I were working on our careers and blindly going through life.

Thankfully, God led us to a Bible-based church where we joined a Bible study group in 2009. We had no idea how important the lessons we were learning would be to our spiritual survival – but God knew!

Our pastor presented a new discipleship program to our church that summer. The program was in response to research that had been published detailing the lack of growth in the American church. Our church was certainly no different, or should I say, our family was certainly no different.

Studies have shown that most church-goers do not read their Bibles on a consistent basis. Many do not have a systematic way of growing available to them. Our church body decided to do something about that issue. My husband and I followed God's leading. We joined one of the discipleship groups our church started that fall and began down a path of purposeful study of God's word.

We did not know then how important it would be that we focused on God's plan for us. Nor did we know how we would need to have God's love for us hidden in our hearts. God knew. We were obedient to His calling to study and He was faithful to fill our hearts with His love.

We read in Psalms many times about how David and the other writers leaned on God in times of peril during the storms of life. Psalm 119:105 tells us *His word is like a lamp that will light our path.*

The storms of this world bring many challenges, but one of the biggest of those challenges is the loss of power, especially the loss of electricity. Our modern world is very dependent on electricity to light our rooms, provide heating and cooling, and even provide information through television and radio programming. A big storm can bring strong winds, ice, heavy rain and/or snow that can all interfere with the ability to see and be informed.

The same is true of storms in our lives. The challenges storms bring can make it difficult to see our path if we start relying on our own abilities instead of the power that can be found in the One who provides true peace and direction. Just like Peter, we need to keep our eyes on God to weather the storm.

Most of us prepare for storms by gassing up power generators or making sure our flashlights have good batteries. Hiding God's word in our hearts is much the same as it provides the light we need when storms hit and we cannot see through the darkness. *Oh, how I love the Word of the Lord and the lessons He hides in my heart.*

God's power lights this world. God's power provides knowledge of how to weather the storms. God's power is all one needs to survive, and we find that power in His word, the Bible.

The Book of Job tells of the wonderful power of our God during the relentless testing of a Godly man. It reminds us that God is *all-knowing* and is *ever present*. If Job, a man that God considered one of his most faithful, can be tested with so many challenges; why in the world would I think I won't be tested?

When I am tested, I must remember that God is always with me. Job 36:4 tells us:

> "For truly my words are not false; One who is perfect in knowledge is with you."

I lean on that lesson because it is hidden in my heart. It is hidden there because I was obedient and studied God's Word when he told me to do so.

Much like Job (and, no – I do not consider myself to be as faithful as Job, but I am working on it), my family and I have been tested in many ways. I wish I could say that we've always looked for God and trusted that He would lead us through any challenge. Unfortunately, that would simply not be a true statement. However, we are growing stronger in our ability to look for God in any challenge or storm and trust He will see us through. *We are looking for the light to show us the path.*

Speaking of the light, the Book of Exodus is an excellent example of God lighting the way. Even though God had already demonstrated His power over and over again, the Hebrews still doubted. God literally provided a *"cloud by day"* and a *"pillar of fire by night"* to show them the way. Yet, at the very first chance they forgot who was leading them. He wasn't hidden in their heart, and the moment He wasn't '*standing before them*', they strayed.

We are all human and subject to forget who God is and what He is. We must be diligent in our seeking of Him in good times and bad. He is always there but, just as Peter did, we need to call out to Him in our moment of need. He will catch us and show us His power.

As I started to reflect on the challenges our family faced, it was easy to recount the storms of 2012 but, in all honesty, the storms had been raging for years. God had been protecting and preparing us all that time. He sought us and brought us close to Himself so we could survive when the 'hurricane' struck that year. I am so thankful He pursued us and drew us close so we could know Him.

Paul tells us in 2 Corinthians 4:6,

> "For it is the God who commanded light to shine out of darkness, who has shone in our hearts to give the light of the knowledge of the glory of God in the face of Jesus Christ."

The knowledge of Him is the light that shines. God spoke light into this world and He continues to make it shine for us. There is light even in darkness. There is love even in storms.

Chapter 3

Ignoring The Forecast

> [5] Trust in the LORD with all your heart,
> And lean not on your own understanding;
> [6] In all your ways acknowledge Him,
> And He shall direct your paths.
> Proverbs 3:5-6

The Book of Proverbs is filled with many wise words of advice. It is filled with many warnings about what to do and what not to do. Such simple instructions should be easy to follow, but the obvious is not always so to those who do not want to hear or know.

I was working for a project management company in early 2011. I had been there about five years and had seen a lot of changes with that firm. Many of those changes included opportunities for learning and growing in my career. The owners of the company decided to sell it to a larger firm in late 2010. This meant more changes would be coming, and I was looking forward to the future.

My boss took me out for lunch one day in early 2011. He presented me with a token of appreciation for my years of hard work and dedication which I used to take my family on a vacation that Spring. He also told me how his role with the company would be changing and that it was his intention to move me from Operations Manager to General Manager by the end of the year. I was humbled and flattered as well as scared, but I welcomed the challenge. The year continued on and I was trying to learn all I could to be prepared when the day would come that I would be responsible for much more.

My boss took me out for lunch again that Summer. This time it was to tell me about his friend's brother who was recently laid-off and looking for work. As it turned out, this man had been a General Manager in his previous role so my boss decided to offer him the position at our company. He told me how it would be a good thing and how I would be able to learn a lot from this man.

At first I was relieved because the prospect of having all of the responsibilities on my shoulders was daunting, but as I thought about the announcement, I began to feel hurt. I had been offered the opportunity and now it had been taken away from me. My pride was getting in the way of change.

I cautioned my boss about the impact this change could have on our team and prepared myself to support the new General Manager. As it turned out, things did not go well and there was a lot of turmoil on the team. Looking back I can see areas where I was less than supportive and certainly not acting in a way that would honor God.

However, I cannot take all of the blame for what would happen the week before Christmas 2011. There is no glory in recounting the details, but the end result was a disagreement between the new General Manager and me. I went home two days before Christmas knowing I would not be going back.

I was unemployed for the first time in my adult career life. I was unemployed not by my choice. My pride was shattered. I had placed too much of my identity into that job and had to reassess what was important and why.

God had been trying to get my attention for quite a while, but I didn't want to let go of that idol. My husband saw the unhealthiness of my situation at that company, but I wasn't willing to let go. That job was not what I did for a living – *it had become who I thought I was.*

The Bible warns us many times about putting our trust, faith and identity in to the wrong things. We are warned that storms will rise in our lives and we need to have our eyes fixed on the One who supplies all of our needs, not on our abilities, other people or the places and things of this world. It is so easy to lose focus on the One that never leaves us when we move our eyes off of Him.

Many are familiar with the stories of faith found in Hebrews 11, but it is verses 39 and 40 that jump out at me. After the long list of examples of God's providing for people of such great faith, we are told they did not receive the promise. All of the people listed in Hebrews 11 experienced God's faithfulness in their lives. He brought them to and, most of the time, through great trials. Even so, they did not see the promise. They did not live to know the *ONE* that can save them from their humanity.

We are blessed to be on this side of the cross. We are blessed to be able to read about and study the life of Jesus Christ. We are blessed to be able to know Him and know that He suffered as we suffer and yet He did not give in to temptation.

I am blessed to know that He was tempted with the opportunity to rule this world – by man's definition – and yet He did not fall to that temptation. I know what it is to be tempted in that way, but I did not resist as Christ did. I also know what it is for God to stay by my side to bring me through that failure polished and more aware than before I strayed. *Oh, how faithful He is!*

God knows all, especially our hearts. He knows what is best for us and gives us opportunities to follow His leading, but many times we resist because we are afraid of the challenge or perhaps we don't want to follow. I was so focused on my plans I could not see that God was leading me somewhere else. As Jonah found out, and so did I, you can run but you cannot hide from the plans of the Lord.

God knew exactly what was coming, and He was trying to get my attention for a long while. He finally pulled the rug out from under me and made me go even though my pride made me want to stay at a job that was clearly not good for me. I had to go into the 'belly of the fish' and it stunk.

The Book of Jonah tells us the story of God directing Jonah to go to Nineveh and warn them to turn from their sins. Jonah didn't want to go to Nineveh because he didn't want them to be saved from their sins. Jonah tried to run from the LORD and went so far as to board a ship heading the other way. God knew where he was and what he was trying to do so God sent a great storm that almost broke the ship apart.

Jonah had to confess to the others on board that he was the reason the storm arose, and he told them to toss him overboard. The men on the ship didn't want to toss him over. They tried hard to save themselves and Jonah, but the storm kept raging. Eventually, they had no choice but to toss him into the water.

I believe the same is true for my experience at that company. I don't think my former boss wanted to toss me overboard, but he was caught in a bad spot. Yes, he had made choices that made it difficult for me to stay but, if I'm honest, I really needed to go. As I said before, the situation was not healthy for me and mostly by my own doing. I needed to be tossed over the side because I was trying to run and hide from the direction God was leading.

As I said earlier, this was the beginning of the storm. Unlike Jonah, the waters did not calm once I was tossed out of the boat, but God's plan was taking shape and I was certainly along for the ride. I cried out to God because things weren't going according to my plan. He loved me anyway. He kept steering the ship and moving me toward where I needed to be to survive the approaching storm.

The Bible tells us that storms will come when we don't listen. We are told the story of a series of storms that rose up because a group of men did not listen to Paul. He had been arrested and was being taken to Rome.

In Acts 27, Paul warned his captors not to sail their ship, but they didn't listen. As a result, they were hit with several severe storms and feared all would be lost. They tossed everything over one-by-one before he comforted their fears and told them they will lose the ship and everything on it but would not lose their lives. They should have listened to him in the beginning, but they didn't. There would be a consequence but there would also be protection.

We are told in Philippians 4 how we should live. Reading it again I am reminded that God provides all, even direction in how to proceed each day. We should look for Him, trust in Him, and He will guide our way. The problems of life, the storms of life arise when we take our eyes off Him and ignore the warning signs. The radar tells us a storm is coming but we head out to sea anyway. That is when we find ourselves in trouble and the ship starts to rock back and forth.

Chapter 4

The Storm Starts To Roll

> ⁶Be strong and of good courage, do not fear nor be afraid of them;
> For the Lord your God, He is the One who goes with you.
> He will not leave you nor forsake you.
> Deuteronomy 31:6

We are told in Deuteronomy that God will be always with us. Moses was speaking to Joshua and encouraged him to carry on even though Moses would not be going with them in to the Promised Land. Joshua had been with Moses for forty years in the desert and was now looking at the land that had been promised, but he would have to go in to that land without his mentor.

Moses again encouraged Joshua, this time in front of all of Israel in Deuteronomy 31:7-8,

> "Then Moses called Joshua and said to him in the sight of all Israel, 'Be strong and of good courage, for you must go with this people to the land which the Lord has sworn to their fathers to give them, and you shall cause them to inherit it. And the Lord, He is the One who goes before

you. He will be with you. He will not leave you nor forsake you; do not fear nor be dismayed.'"

I find it interesting the number of times God has to give us the same message over and over before we finally understand. Even then, we can easily forget that He is always with us. God has a plan for our lives, and He is working that plan for His good. We simply need to trust that He is faithful and will always be with us. We need to find peace even when the storms around us make no sense.

Looking back it's easy to see the plan God was working out, but it was hidden from me at the time. Even though we had to go through difficult times, I am grateful that He did have a plan. God put me exactly where I needed to be and within six weeks of losing my previous job, I started a new one with much less stress, closer to home, great benefits, and the same pay. Although I was actively searching for a new job, I did not find this one – it found me. God's wonderful plan was at work.

I started my new job on February 15, 2012. Four weeks later, as I was settling in learning all there ever was to know about parking meters, my husband called to tell me he'd gotten a call from his boss advising him that his position had been eliminated. He would lose his job at the end of March.

We told ourselves we weren't worried about that change because we had decided to start our own business when I lost my job. Now my husband would be able to take over the reins while he started looking for his next opportunity. We were trusting that God's plan was still at work but worry was still lurking in the shadows. I was still new in my job and now my husband was looking for work. We were trusting God but not leaning on Him. We were working our plan.

Sometimes storms come one after another and without much warning. The Bible tells us in the books of Matthew, Mark, and Luke of a storm that rolled in and frightened the disciples while they were crossing the sea with Jesus.

> "And suddenly a great tempest arose on the sea, so that the boat was covered with the waves. But He was asleep." (Matthew 8:24)

The writers tell us the disciples woke Jesus and He immediately calmed the sea. Matthew and Luke report the disciples 'marveled' at Jesus' ability to calm the sea, but Mark tells us they "feared exceedingly." They questioned one another in Mark 4:41[b] asking,

> "Who can this be, that even the wind and sea obey Him?"

Why is it that we are often surprised when storms rush in? Don't we know they are going to happen? And, when they do happen, don't we know our God is stronger than any storm?

All was moving forward, or so we thought, until early one morning in May when the telephone rang. My son's high school was calling to report there had been an issue at school and our presence was required. This was certainly not the way I wanted to start that day!

We went to the school to deal with the issue at hand, grateful that it happened the day before my son's eighteenth birthday. He would lose a week of school, the privilege of attending Senior Prom and walking in graduation, but would be awarded a high school diploma as long as he completed all of his work. It was disappointing for this mother to not see her son walk in cap and gown to be presented with his diploma, but our focus for the next six weeks was primarily on making sure he earned that piece of paper. As a parent, we understood the high school diploma was just a beginning, but it is the foundation for many choices that will come later in life. He did earn his diploma. God's plan was still working.

We spent the next several weeks dealing with the fall-out from the issue at school that morning but life went on. It was now Summer and we were busy keeping things together, paying bills, and trying to get our business off the ground. We continued in our Bible study and were trying to keep our focus on the things we could control and learning to let go of the things we couldn't. I wish I could say that I understood the difference, but I certainly did not. I had let go of the idol of work but had latched on even tighter to the idol of my children.

Out of respect for my son, I will not share many of the details of the challenges we were facing that summer. I truly believe it is his story to tell if and when he decides he wants to tell it. However, I will confess that I was not setting a good example of Christ's love to him or his brothers as we traveled through that challenging time.

There is no one that can cast doubt on the love I have for our sons. I gave birth to three of them and was blessed to gain two more by marriage to my husband. We love them all by the same measure but not all in the same way. They are different people, and our love for them reflects our relationships with them.

Speaking only of the three sons I was blessed to bring into this world: one is strong and confident, one is loving and caring, and the third is driven and seeks acceptance. They are a product of our love for them and their choices in life, but our love cannot chart the course their lives will take. They must make their own decisions and, as a result, create their own path. My only hope and prayer for them is and has always been that they will know God and follow Him. They all do in some ways, but not the way I want for them. I had to learn and accept that they have a God who loves them and wants good things for them. *I am not their God! Ouch!*

The Bible tells us in Proverbs 22:6 that we are to,

> "Train up a child in the way he should go, and
> when he is old he will not depart from it."

We tried to do just that but, it seemed like our sons were going their own way. Why weren't they just following us? Hadn't we shown them the way to go? Actually, the answer to that question was that we hadn't, but we weren't ready to face that yet.

I was trying to hang on to my son as tightly as I could while thinking that I could protect him from the evils of this world. My actions and decisions didn't come out of a desire to harm him or keep him from good things. In fact, I wanted to protect him from making bad choices or mistakes that could harm him for years to come – even for eternity. *If only he would do what I wanted him to do all would be OK.* At least, that is what I thought.

I held on tighter and tighter as time went on, but the tighter I gripped the more he pulled away. He had to make his own way in this world. He had to make his own choices and feel the consequences of those choices. He had to feel the pain of falling down before he could experience the accomplishment of walking on his own. *I let him learn to walk when he was a toddler, why couldn't I do it now?*

Most of us are familiar with the story of the prodigal son from Luke Chapter 15. We read about the choice the father made to honor the desire of his son by giving him his inheritance and letting him go. We also read about the father's joy when he sees his son coming back. I know the point of the parable is to understand God the Father's joy when we return to Him, but I cannot help but think about how hard it must be on God to wait for us to return.

Jesus tells the story about the struggles the son went through after leaving the father's house, but He doesn't tell about the father's struggles waiting for his son to return. What patience it must have taken to allow this child whom he loved so much to wander until he came to the knowledge that life with his father is better than life without.

I cannot say that I had patience during those months in the summer of 2012. I didn't. I was doing everything I could to keep my son *with* me instead of letting him go into the hands of the One who wanted so desperately to reach him. I had to get out of the way and let God protect him and direct him.

We were blessed to be attending a discipleship group that was focused on studying God's Word and applying it to our lives. A very wise and loving woman also belonged to our small group of seven. The advice she gave me that summer has stuck with me even years later and was eye-opening to how I was '*managing*' the situation.

You see, I had been trying to control my son. I thought I had all of the answers he needed. If only he would listen and do what I told him to do. But God had another plan for him. He had another path He wanted my son to take and I had to let go. I was in a tug-of-war with God and my son was the rope. I was getting burned day and night. The burning would continue until I let go of the rope.

I was so consumed by my desire to control my youngest son that I didn't see the good things happening with the rest of my family. Way too often we tend to focus on things that are not in our control and miss out on the blessings this world brings. My story that summer was not much different.

My oldest had returned from Iraq safely to his base in Hawaii. My husband and I were attending our discipleship group and continuing to grow closer to the Lord. As a result of the lessons we had been learning and a desire to be obedient to God, my husband decided to follow the Lord in believer's baptism. He and my middle son were baptized in August.

My husband and I would join our church a month later. We had been attending for almost eight years. I had been praying for a long time that God would lead my husband to become a member of that church. He did and His plan continued to work, but all I could see was the one that I couldn't control. I missed the joys and blessings around me because I was so focused on a problem that wasn't mine to solve.

Chapter 5

The Boat Rocks And Changes Course

> ¹³but rejoice to the extent that you partake of Christ's sufferings,
> that when His glory is revealed,
> you may also be glad with exceeding joy.
> 1 Peter 4:13

We are told in 1 Peter that we are to rejoice in suffering. I cannot – and will not – equate any trial or challenge we face in this world to the suffering our Savior endured for us on the cross. But, I will say I have learned to find reason to rejoice in life's suffering. It didn't happen all at once and it didn't happen overnight, but it did happen for us. It can happen for you, too, if you learn to trust Him in all the storms life may bring you.

It's been said the enemy cannot take away our salvation. This is true but he can try to make us stumble. He can put people, places and things in our path that cause us to take our eyes off God. The Book of Job tells us about several struggles Satan put into Job's life. Satan tried everything he could to cause Job to turn from God. God allowed the trials to befall on Job because he knew Job's heart.

God knew Job loved and trusted in Him but this didn't mean that Job did not stumble. Job 30:20-23 gives us a glimpse into the despair Job was feeling. He cries out to God but gets no answer. Job feels that God is against him because He is not rescuing him. We read in verse 21,

> "But You have become cruel to me; with the strength of Your hand You oppose me."

Job even says that he feels death will be the result of the challenges before him. Job didn't know why things were happening. He felt God had deserted him or was against him. God loved Job and was watching all of the time.

The enemy had been trying hard during the first nine months of 2012 to cause my husband and me to stumble. We remained faithful and continued to grow in the truth of the love of God. Satan's stumbling blocks had not taken our eyes off God. Satan had to move to move on to a higher gear. Things were about to get even more stormy than they had ever been.

It was Monday, October 1st and we were watching television when my youngest son sent me a text. He was letting me know he was out with friends and would not be home that night. I thanked him for letting me know and set about with the activities of my evening. I locked the front door, took my shower and went to bed.

Our family had been through many challenges during the previous months, actually years, with my son. I was grateful he reached out to let me know in advance that he would not be coming home. This saved me lost hours of sleep waiting for the door to open at whatever hour he would decide to grace our home with his presence.

I was sound asleep when the telephone rang at 1:30 AM. Most calls at this hour do not bring happy news. This was not to be an exception, but God was still working His plan.

I jumped out of bed at the sound of my cell phone ringing. I saw from the Caller ID that it was my son's cell phone number calling me, so I fully expected to hear his voice on the other end when I answered. I expected something along the lines of, *"Mom, I messed up and need you to come get me."* However, my son's voice was not the one I heard that morning.

The voice I heard was that of his friend telling me something was wrong with my son. The next voice was the police officer asking me medical questions about my son and telling me the situation was serious. I needed to get over there quickly. I woke my husband and son to have him take me over to the friend's house. We arrived as they were bringing my youngest son out of the house on a stretcher.

His brother and I met the ambulance at the hospital. I spent the night in the Emergency Room with my youngest child. The next day and a half would be spent at his bedside in the hospital room as the reality of what happened brought our next steps into focus. After much prayer for answers and directions, God had brought us to this place. The choice was not an easy one, but it was what needed to be done at that time.

My son and I had a long talk on the way home from the hospital that Wednesday afternoon. I told him how much we loved him but we could not continue on the path that we'd been on for the previous two and a half years. He needed to make a choice and would need to advise us of his choice the next day.

I went to work on Thursday. I was still new in my position and needed to protect my job. My husband was still looking to replace his and our business was just starting to take off. My husband called around 3:30 to let me know my son was not at home. I called him but he didn't answer so I sent a text to my son's cell phone.

He answered with, *"I'm hanging out with friends and won't be home tonight. See you later."* I was disappointed with that answer and advised him this was not the choice we had hoped he would make. He needed to stop by the house to pick up his clothes and medicine.

My son came by the house that night to get his medication. It would be the last time we would see him for almost two weeks. Those were two of the longest weeks of this mother's life.

I cannot say I did not know where he was because we could, and did, track his cell phone but we did not speak for those twelve days. His father eventually called on Tuesday evening October 16th to say that our son had reached out to him asking to move to Iowa. Our son needed a place to stay until he could make arrangements to get him out there. My son was back in my house within minutes and my husband set about finding airline tickets to get him out of New Jersey.

I went to work the next day but took the afternoon off to take my son to the hospital. He had a hospital bill that needed to be addressed before he left. To put it mildly, my son was not a *'happy camper'* about the cost of an ambulance ride, the doctors' services, and two days in the hospital. He was strongly voicing his opinion – actually, yelling – on the ride home when my oldest son called.

I answered the call using the speaker phone in the car. My youngest son was carrying on about the criminals at the hospital while my oldest son and I tried to calm him down. Eventually, he blurted out something I didn't expect.

"Well, you don't know what it's like to have your friend killed!"

God's timing is so perfect and his work is complete. There is no one in this world that could have fielded that comment any better than my oldest son.

Without missing a beat and without a moment's hesitation, Ray replied, "Well, actually I do. I was standing next to him. Were you?"

My son Ray was serving in the US Army and was only a few months back from being stationed in Iraq. His unit was sent to Iraq in July 2010. The next month the President of the United States would announce that combat operations in Iraq had ceased; however, my son's unit would stay on for several more months. It wouldn't take long for my son's life to change – just over a month.

My son's unit was stationed in Northern Iraq, but he couldn't tell me where. I was at work when I kept getting a call on my cell phone from a number I didn't recognize. My husband was getting a call from the same number. Our pastor called my husband and told him he had just spoken with our son and we needed to answer the call the next time it came across.

It wasn't long and my cell phone rang again. This time I answered it and heard the sound of my son's voice on the other end. Ray was 25 years old at the time but sounded like he had aged 20 years. He still couldn't tell me where he was but he wanted to let me know he was alive. His unit had been attacked by an Iraqi soldier and two of his fellow soldiers were killed. Ray was shaken but alive.

Fast-forward to 2012 and the call taking place in my car. As I said, there was no one on this earth who could have fielded the question my youngest threw out better than his oldest brother. God allowed that call to happen exactly when and how it did.

Silence! Complete silence in the car! It was not a normal practice for Ray to call at that time. He was stationed in Hawaii and it was mid-morning there but God knew exactly what was going to happen and who could handle it best. God's plan at work again!

The Scriptures tell us many times that we are to trust in God's plan. The question is often asked, *"How are we to ask for God's plan?"* Well, Jesus modeled the way we are to pray in Matthew 6:9-13:

"In this manner, therefore, pray:

> Our Father in heaven,
> Hallowed be Your name.
> Your kingdom come.
> Your will be done
> On earth as it is in heaven.
> Give us this day our daily bread.
> And forgive us our debts,
> As we forgive our debtors.
> And do not lead us into temptation,

> But deliver us from the evil one.
> For Yours is the kingdom and the power and the
> glory forever. Amen."

We are also given this prayer in Luke 11. Most people refer to this prayer as The Lord's Prayer. Others call it The Disciples' Prayer because Jesus instructed his disciples to pray in this manner. No matter what you may call it, we are to pray for God's will to be done.

Many of us have prayed that prayer but few realize what a powerful statement it is to say – *and believe* – that God's will is best. The saying part is easy. The believing and executing parts are scary because that means we have to trust God's plan for us and our loved ones is better than any plan we could conceive, even if the workings of that plan don't make sense in the here and now.

How can letting go of my son show him I love him? I can't explain it, but it is what God wanted us to do at the time.

We put my two youngest sons on a plane that Thursday morning and sent them to Iowa. I hugged my son and told him I loved him. I didn't know if or when we would speak again but I had to trust that God was working His plan in my son's life. God loves him more than I can ever know and that had to be enough for me.

My middle child happily escorted his brother and welcomed the trip to see his father and family but had to return a week later. He was a member of the New Jersey Air National Guard and he had orders. There was a storm coming.

Chapter 6

Running From The Storm

> ²⁴And suddenly a great tempest arose on the sea,
> so that the boat was covered with the waves.
> But He was asleep.
> Matthew 8:24

I find it interesting the number of times we read about troubles in the Bible but it seems like God is just resting. Matthew, Mark and Luke all tell us about the storm that rose up on the Sea of Galilee as Jesus and the disciples crossed. What was Jesus doing while the boat was being tossed to and fro? He was sleeping.

Sleeping? Didn't He care about the peril everyone was in?

Sleeping? Didn't He know how frightened the men were as the boat was being tossed about?

Yes, He did know but He also knew His power, and He knew they would be OK. Jesus knew He was here to serve a purpose and that purpose was not to die by drowning in a storm on that sea. But the disciples didn't know this, so they worried. They were so worried they woke Him up and begged Him to save them. Save them He did.

This is where things really started to get stormy for us! Most people, especially those in the Mid-Atlantic and Northeast who think of storms in 2012, are reminded of Hurricane Sandy (also known as Superstorm Sandy) that hit New Jersey, New York, and other states on October 29, 2012. As it turns out, my biggest storm that year would coincide with Sandy, but it would not be the natural disaster that would bring about the major change in our lives. Just like the hurricane, this storm had been brewing for some time and it hit on October 29th. It brought with it pain and fear but it also brought the greatest peace I've ever known.

Like I said, the storm had been coming on for a long while before it actually hit. I had to admit to myself the symptoms I was feeling were not going away and would require some intervention of their own. My family has a long history of heart disease affecting both of my parents and now two of my three brothers. I was having chest pains and shortness of breath. I knew what these symptoms meant but made many excuses about why I couldn't go to the doctor.

I couldn't go on Thursday night because that was the night my husband and I attended a support group. *The people in that group needed us there for support.*

I couldn't go on Friday night because that was the night my husband and I attended a discipleship/Bible study group. *We needed to be there to grow stronger in the Word.*

I couldn't go on Saturday because my husband and I had purchased tickets to a seminar that Saturday and we certainly didn't want that money to go to waste.

This brought us to Sunday. I definitely couldn't go on Sunday. After all, we had church and my son was coming back from Iowa. *I had to be there to make sure he got home safely.*

We went to church that Sunday morning as usual. I remember having to sit down during the praise songs to catch my breath, and I couldn't clap my hands without pain. The signs were there, but I was still making excuses.

We went home after church and had brunch like we always did on Sundays. We drove to New York City after eating so we could meet my son's train at Penn Station. We had decided to bring him in by train because the hurricane was coming up the East Coast and we weren't sure where or when it would make landfall. New York City was far enough north we thought that he'd be able to get in safely.

My husband parked the car about a block and a half from Penn Station. I had to stop a few times to catch my breath as we walked from the car to the train station. I quickly found a seat to rest in once we made it inside and waited for my son to arrive.

His train came in to the station about twenty minutes before they closed it in preparation for the storm's arrival. He was home and God's plan was still at work.

We stopped for a bite to eat and then went home. I remember coming to terms with the reality of my symptoms that night but the excuses kept coming. Some people say, *"Once a control-freak, always a control-freak."* Well, not so much - but more on that later.

I went about my normal activities of getting ready for bed that night. I finally admitted I would need help but wasn't ready to go get that help yet. So, I said the second dumbest thing I've ever said to myself while I took my shower that night.

"If I make it through the night, I am going to go to work in the morning, get the office ready for the storm, and then I'll have Roger take me to the hospital."

Don't worry, I'll share the dumbest thing in a little bit, but first let me explain what was wrong with this statement. The fact that there was even a question about whether or not I would make it through the night should have resulted in an immediate trip to the hospital, but it didn't. I thought I was in control of the situation, and I had a plan.

I had come to terms with the reality that I had some sort of blockage in my heart. My plan was to go to work on Monday and use the imminent storm to help cover some of the time that would be needed to address the *"issue"* medically. I had it all worked out.

I would go to the hospital after the office closed in preparation of the storm. The doctors would diagnose the blockage and put a stent in to clear the blockage. I would be in the hospital overnight and released on Tuesday. But the office would most likely be closed because of the storm, so I wouldn't miss any time at work. I would return to work on Wednesday without any lost time. Great plan, right? Well, it was not God's plan.

I've admitted to being a recovering *'controlaholic'* – I'll claim that word even if it is not a word. I thought I could plan and control my way through almost anything, even a heart attack. My life had already demonstrated over and over many times how *my plans* rarely worked out well, but I just knew one of these times my plan would be the best plan and would match the plan that God had for me. I just needed to show Him I was right and things could work out my way.

Sometimes we push God so far that He has to jerk us back to reality with something big and dramatic. He wants us to acknowledge *His Power, His Plan, His Will* for our lives and trust Him. When we don't trust in God's plan, we are really saying that we don't trust God.

Even though Job was a man that was *"blameless and upright, and one who feared God and shunned evil"* (Job 1:1), he was not immune to doubt. We read about his doubts and questioning of God several times in the book that bears his name. God allowed Job to be tested and suffer great hardships because he knew Job's heart, but did Job fully know God's heart?

We read about Job's despair in 9:17:

> "For He crushes me with a tempest, and multiplies my wounds without cause."

Wow! Job was suffering and had no idea why. He knew that many bad things had befallen him but couldn't see the end result. How could he? None of it made any sense to him.

Job had tried to live a life that was *"blameless and upright."* He feared God and tried to stay far from evil but evil seemed to have found him. He suffered much more before he came to the point of questioning God's reasons for allowing the bad things to happen.

Job had a plan. Job's plan was to be as good as he could be to earn God's protection. Now that protection was taken away and Job was suffering. Wasn't Job's plan good enough?

No! Job's plan wasn't good enough and neither are our plans. We are supposed to submit to God's will which equates to submitting to God's plan for our lives. We've heard over and over about the need to seek out God's will but, let's be honest, what we really want is for God to do what we want and how we want it done.

I was having a heart attack and knew there was something seriously wrong, but I still thought my plan, my will was better than God's. I allowed my fear of losing my job (not trusting God) to keep me from going to the hospital that Sunday night. I didn't trust God that He could protect me from the fallout of missing work on Monday. So, I suffered pain and put my life and others' lives in jeopardy as a result. God had a plan, and He was going to work *His* plan even if I didn't want to get out of the way.

CHAPTER 7

The Storm Arrives

> [25] For He commands and raises the stormy wind,
> which lifts up the waves of the sea.
> [26] They mount up to the heavens,
> They go down again to the depths;
> Their soul melts because of trouble.
> [27] They reel to and fro, and stagger like a drunken man,
> and are at their wits' end.
> Psalm 107:25-27

God allows life to bring us many challenges. We can try to run from them or we can face them head on. The storm will come despite what we do or don't do.

I've told the story many times to family, friends, and employees about having to face the challenges before us. I like to use the analogy of "*hitting the wall*" because of my history as a long distance runner. You see, we will all be faced with a difficult choice at some time in our lives. If we look at that choice as a "wall," we have to choose from the options in front of us.

We can choose to give in to the wall and turn around.

We can choose to avoid the wall and try to walk around it.

We can choose to scale the wall and climb over it.

Or, we can choose to put our head down and go through the wall.

There are consequences to all of these choices, and which one is right will depend on the situation. Knowing which one is right will be largely dependent on our relationship with God and our trust in His will for our lives.

There was some question about whether I would make it through the night on Sunday. I did make it and went to work that Monday morning. The team and I prepared the office for the storm and we sent everyone home around 11:00. By the time I left, the pain in my arms was so bad I couldn't even hold a telephone to my ear. This didn't stop me from getting in my car to drive home.

We read often about God's love and protection. Psalm 121 tells us that God will help those who seek Him. He protects us even from ourselves. In Verse 7 we read:

> "The LORD shall preserve you from all evil; He shall preserve your soul."

We are further comforted in Verse 8 that the LORD *will watch over our comings and goings for all times.*

I was backing out of my parking space when I called my husband to tell him I would need him to take me to the hospital because I was having a heart attack. My husband is a wise, loving and responsible man. His reply was perfect and justified, "Where are you at? I'll send an ambulance."

My response was not so wise. In fact, it was the dumbest thing I've ever said. "No, *I'm all right.* Just meet me at home."

I'm all right? I just told him I'm having a heart attack.

I'm all right? I couldn't raise my arms to steer the car. I had to drive home using only my thumbs and forefingers on alternating hands resting on my lap because the pain hurt so bad to raise them up.

I am eternally grateful for God's grace that day. He protected me from myself, and He protected everyone else on the road. I had no idea how ignorant that choice was at the time, but I would learn in just a few hours that my plan was not at work. God had a plan, and He was protecting me while it worked out. Yes, God's plan was at work even though I was in pain. He was drawing me closer and closer to Him.

I made it home and parked the car. I got out of the driver's seat and moved to the passenger seat while my husband came out to drive me to the hospital. He had called a friend while waiting for me to get home and was told to take me to the new hospital that had just been opened a few months earlier. Sounded like great advice.

Sometimes we put ourselves in trouble because we listen to advice from others or trust our own advice. I certainly had a tendency to believe that I had the solution to almost any problem and this situation was no different. *How many times would it take before I would finally learn I was not in control?*

The Bible is filled with stories of groups of people that God tried over and over to convince that He was worthy of their trust. He sent Jonah to Nineveh to preach to the people and get them to repent. Despite objections and after unsuccessful attempts at running from this task, Jonah went to Nineveh and preached. They repented. Great, right? Well, the story doesn't end there.

The Book of Nahum tells us that just a few generations later the people of Nineveh had fallen back to their old ways. They weren't trusting and following God. This time God would not be so gentle in getting their attention. We read that God was jealous, furious, and would take vengeance. Nahum 1:3 tells us,

> "The LORD is slow to anger and great in power, and will not at all acquit the wicked. The LORD has His way in the whirlwind and in the storm, and the clouds are the dust of His feet."

The dust was about to fly in my world because I was still trying to work my plan.

We arrived at the hospital and the nurse did a quick EKG which did in fact diagnose there was an issue going on. She gave me the first dose of Nitroglycerin and the pain subsided a little. A few minutes later she gave me the second dose then stepped out of the room for a quick minute.

Shortly after she left the room, I asked my husband to find me a basin. I remember feeling nauseous and thought I was going to be sick. Our pastor and a good friend were in the room with Roger and me. They stepped out of the room as my husband handed me the basin. That is the last thing I remember.

It would be easy to read the passages from Nahum 1 and think that God had stopped caring for the people of Nineveh. I don't believe this is the case and see evidence of His love for them in Nahum 1:7,

> "The LORD is good, a stronghold in the day of trouble; and He knows those who trust in Him."

I never stopped trusting in God, and He never let go of me.

I woke up to a nurse standing over me on my left and a doctor on my right. There was a "crash cart" behind the nurse and my husband was in the corner behind the doctor. The look on my husband's face was filled with fear. The doctor asked me if I knew what just happened. Yes, I did. The "crash cart" only comes in for a few select reasons. My heart had stopped.

A few minutes later the cardiologist arrived. He advised me that the hospital we were at was well equipped for many things and would be a great place to be at if I was having a baby, but it was not equipped for complicated cardiac care. He recommended that I be transferred to the heart hospital in Camden because there was a storm coming and they didn't want me at this hospital if my condition worsened.

Worsened? My heart just stopped! Doesn't get much worse than that!

So, I was loaded in to an ambulance as Hurricane Sandy was making landfall about an hour east of the hospital. I remember the EMT riding in the back with me kept asking how I was feeling and then he would ask the driver how much farther we had to go. I thought he was concerned about the storm outside, but I would learn soon enough it was the storm inside me he was most concerned with during that ride.

We arrived at Our Lady of Lourdes Hospital in Camden, NJ that afternoon, and I was brought in to a room in the Cardiac Care Unit. There were doctors and nurses and technicians all around me getting me settled in for the night. The decision had been made to keep me there and do the heart catheterization in the morning. I settled in and listened to the storm as it blew through New Jersey.

I couldn't sleep so I decided to call my son in Hawaii around 2:00 AM. He was the only one I thought would be up at that time of night since it really wasn't night yet in Hawaii. I spoke to him for a little bit, told him I loved him and not to worry. Everything was going to be all right. I still thought things would go according to my plan – a little altered – but basically my plan. God had a different plan, and He was working it out.

Chapter 8

Finding Peace In The Storm

> ²⁸Then they cry out to the Lord in their trouble,
> And He brings them out of their distresses.
> ²⁹He calms the storm,
> So that its waves are still.
> Psalm 107:28-29

I wish I could say after all I had experienced I learned to trust in God's will. I wish it because it was not so. Not yet! I still thought my plan would work. It would be a modified version of my plan but I still had faith in the plan I had worked out.

It is hard to let go of the plans we have for ourselves and to truly trust God. As I've said before, it is easy to *say* we trust God but not so easy to *live out*. Truly submitting to God's will and giving up all efforts to define the outcome for ourselves is very difficult to do because it can feel like you have no control. I have a secret to share here – *you don't have control*.

We trick ourselves into believing that we can change things in our lives if we just work hard enough at it. I spent many years in a profession that was centered on controlling people and outcomes that were out of my reach. I thought I could do the same with my family and with my life. I was trying to project manage every aspect of my surroundings and it simply was not working out the way I had carefully planned for it to go.

Now, let me be clear here: *I am not a victim*. I made choices in my life that definitely affected my health. Genetics played a big role in the situation I was living that October day, but I cannot blame genetics for the timing or the severity of the condition I was in.

I had refused to listen to the warnings and make the changes that had been laid out for me. I may not have been able to save myself from the medical diagnosis I had to face that day, but I certainly could have done things differently had I listened. Listening may have lessened the severity of my diagnosis and it may have even delayed it. I hadn't listened because I thought I was in control, and I had a plan.

Jesus gives us the ultimate example of letting go of control and submitting to the Father's will. I cannot imagine the torment and grief our Savior must have been feeling as He considered the events that were about to occur. In Mark 14:36 and again in Luke 22:42, Jesus lets go of His fears and trusts in the Father's plan. He prayed,

> "Father, if it is Your will, take this cup away from Me; nevertheless not My will, but Yours be done."

Wow – now that is true submission to God's plan. If only I could have found the courage to trust the Father's plan earlier, I may have avoided this life changing event. I didn't and so God used it to bring about the change He knew I needed in my life.

The nurses came to get me around 6:00 AM that morning. They took me down to the surgical room so the surgeon could do his work. I was familiar with the angioplasty procedure because my parents and brother had been through them before me. I knew the risks and expected the doctor to insert a stent (maybe two) and we'd be on our way back to life as normal. What I didn't expect was that my first trip in for angioplasty would not be able to fix my problems and it would not be my last. More on the return visits later but first we must deal with the reality that came into focus that morning.

As the doctor began the procedure, I was trying to watch his progress on the screens in the room. Yes, I thought if I could see what he was doing I would have some sort of control. The truth is God was in control and I was just going along for the ride.

The doctor finished his procedure and then came up to talk to me. He put his hand on my shoulder and told me he would not be able to fix my issues with a stent – or even two – because I had multiple blockages and needed open heart surgery for cardiac bypass. Open heart surgery was certainly not in my plans, but it was part of God's plan.

The team of doctors and nurses finished the procedure and moved me back to my room. The doctor told my husband it would be a few days before they would schedule me for the surgery, so we were trying to comfort and encourage each other when the nurse rushed in to the room around 1:00 that afternoon. She asked me to rate my pain level which I did. She left and then came back to tell me I would be going in for surgery that day. The next thing I knew there was a team of nurses getting me ready for this major surgery.

I begged my husband to get my son there before they took me down to the operating room. Fortunately, his base was closed that day due to the storm damage and he was already on his way back. He arrived at the hospital right before they took me in for surgery. I was able to tell my husband, son, step-son and his fiancé that I loved them. I told them not to worry. All would be OK. I really, truly believed everything would be well.

You may wonder how I could be so certain that all would be well. The old me would have wondered that, too. I would have no control over what was about to happen to me. In fact, *I had no control and in that I had all that I needed – God's love and protection.*

We read in Isaiah 43:2,

> "When you pass through the waters, I will be with you; and through the rivers, they shall not overflow you. When you walk through the fire, you shall not be burned, nor shall the flame scorch you."

Those words were very comforting to me knowing that I was not alone. I am so thankful that the knowledge of God's love for me was hidden in my heart, the heart that was about to be stopped and repaired in an operating room in Camden, NJ that October day.

There is a famous poem that comes to mind when I think about the peace I felt that day. In the poem "Footprints in the Sand", the author tells the story of a dream reflecting on her life. She notes in the poem that there were two sets of footprints during good times in her life but only one set during times of struggles. She questions the Lord about why He would abandon her during those times when she needed Him the most. His answer is exactly what I felt that day.

I know what it feels like to have God carry me. He gently lifted me up and carried me in His hands when I needed Him most. He cradled me in His arms, and I felt a sense of peace that truly does pass all understanding.

Psalm 29:11 tells us,

> "The Lord will give strength to His people; the Lord will bless His people with peace."

I wish I had given up my attempts at control long before because there is power in giving in to the peace that only the Lord can give. We read about it. We study it. We don't fully benefit from it until we truly believe in it.

My husband and I had begun a discipleship program a few years earlier. The lessons I learned and the growth in my faith came to full fruition that day as I faced open heart surgery. God longed for me to give in to His will and for me to stop trying to control everything and everyone in my life. Unfortunately, it took a major life challenge before I realized how much God loves me and wants to lead my life. There was nothing like having my chest opened up and my heart taken out to show me that I had so little control and needed to trust God with everything in my life.

Peace. Love. Comfort. Those are the last things I remember feeling as I was wheeled away from my family and back to the operating room. Just as we read in Psalm 107:29, God *will* calm the storm in our lives and make the waves still. We just need to rest in His arms.

The feeling I felt that day was one of being cradled by our LORD. He reached down and carried me through the storm. He lifted me gently and held me closely as the surgeon did his work. God's plan was being carried out, and I was protected through it all.

Chapter 9

Standing After The Storm

> ¹⁴but whoever drinks of the water that I
> shall give him will never thirst.
> But the water that I shall give him will become in him
> a fountain of water springing up into everlasting life.
> John 4:14

We try and fail many times to put the concepts of God's love and provision into human terms. We limit Him with options and solutions we know and have access to when trying to solve our problems. The issue with doing so is that God's ways are so much better than ours, and He wants to give us more than we can ever imagine.

When we are faced with struggles (storms) in this life, He wants to give us peace as He works through the struggle to bring us closer to Himself. It is such a waste of precious time and energy to worry about things we cannot control instead of focusing on the work God wants to do in us. We are told to come to Him, trust Him, and He will be our source of life's living water.

The first thing I remember after surgery was waking up to my nurse Eric telling me to take a deep breath. He told me to blow out as hard as I could as he removed my breathing tube. *Who knew breathing could be so hard?* Our bodies do it naturally and automatically all day and night. We don't have to think about it. It just happens.

It may seem difficult to believe, but I actually had to tell myself to breathe in and breathe out. Every breath I took required a deliberate choice. What option did I have? Well there was really no other option since I had to breathe, but it hurt. My chest hurt. My lungs hurt. I was so tired, but I was alive. God had seen me through, but He still expected me to do my part.

The writers of the Psalms tell us many times that we can lean on God when we are tired. Psalm 46:1 says,

> "God is our refuge and strength, a very present help in trouble."

It was God's strength that allowed me to endure the fatigue and pain that followed the life saving surgery I needed. God spared my life and He wanted me to live it.

Speaking of "living life," God wanted me to learn lessons from my experience. He wanted me to learn *who* and *what* really mattered in this world. He wanted me to put my focus on the important things and let go of those that either don't matter or aren't mine to control.

I remember the television being on in my room. The news coverage showed the devastation at the Jersey Shore and I was especially struck by the images of the Seaside Heights' roller coaster in the ocean. I was brought back to a conversation I had with a customer the week before the storm.

They were a customer of the company I worked for at the time and were trying to prepare their new parking meters for the arrival of the storm. This is when they discovered the wrong locks were sent for the meter covers. He called me looking for a solution. Our vendor had sent the wrong locks. I apologized but could not get the new locks to him before the storm would arrive on Monday.

Seeing the coverage of the roller coaster in the ocean reminded me of the power of nature. If the storm could pick up a roller coaster and place it in the ocean, what difference did it make what locks were on the covers that were on those parking meters? Some disasters in life can be stopped or minimized, some cannot. We need to do what we can and trust God to keep us safe throughout all the storms of life. *Only He can truly provide the shelter we need.*

We often tend to focus and obsess on the things of this world, forgetting they are temporary. Things come and go. People in our lives may come and go, but our God remains forever. He has plans for us and wants us to focus on His plans and not our own.

Jeremiah 29:11 tells us of those plans and the need to have our focus right.

> "For I know the thoughts that I think toward you, says the Lord, thoughts of peace and not of evil, to give you a future and a hope."

Our thoughts are not His thoughts. Our worries are not His worries. Our plans are not His plans. His are much bigger.

Matthew 6:31 tells us to keep perspective on what we should concern ourselves about in life.

> "Therefore do not worry, saying, 'What shall we eat?' or 'What shall we drink?' or 'What shall we wear?'"

This does not mean we are not to concern ourselves about anything, but rather we are not to worry about things we cannot control. The list of things we can control is so much smaller than the list of things we should trust God to control.

So, what do we do with the things we cannot control? Is it reasonable to ask that we forget about all of them? No, of course not, but it is reasonable and expected that we would take them to God and leave them there. We are told in James 1:6,

> "But let him ask in faith, with no doubting, for he who doubts is like a wave of the sea driven and tossed by the wind."

We are to ask and believe an answer will come. It may not come immediately, but it will come.

A day or so after I awoke from surgery, I was moved back to the room I had been in the night I arrived at the hospital. At some point I noticed a water tower off in the distance. The water tower had been there through the storm and it looked like it had seen several storms. It was leaning and was certainly not in use, but the fact that it was still standing struck me as I looked out at my "friend" the water tower.

I thought about how Christ tells us to come to him when we thirst. He is the true water of life and will be there for us through all of life's storms.

Isaiah 55 is filled with commands and encouragement to come to God for all of our needs. We are told,

> "Everyone who thirsts, come to the waters."

The chapter continues on with ways that God meets our needs but He asks that we seek Him. He will be there throughout all storms. He will provide in ways we cannot know or imagine. He is faithful and just wants us to look for - and to - Him.

Jesus tells us again of the importance of coming to Him when we thirst and need water. He said in John 7:37[b]-38,

> "If anyone thirsts, let him come to Me and drink. He who believes in Me, as the Scripture has said, out of his heart will flow rivers of living water."

Jesus provides all that we need and will be there through all of the storms of life. We just need to seek Him, trust Him, and share His love to realize the benefit of having a fully healed heart. Surgeons can fix the vessels in our human hearts but only God can heal us of our true sickness. We have to trust in God's plan and seek Him out to realize the full blessings that can be ours.

CHAPTER 10

Another Storm, Another Lesson

> ⁷In my distress I called upon the LORD,
> And cried out to my God;
> He heard my voice from His temple,
> And my cry entered His ears.
> 2 Samuel 22:7

God had seen me through a challenging storm. He brought me through the storm and sheltered me as the healing process began. More storms would come before the end of the year, but first I needed to heal. Healing included rest and renewal followed by life back to normal, but normal was not going to be the same.

My stay at the hospital would be typical for recovery after open-heart surgery. I entered the hospital on a Monday and was released the next Monday. My husband knew I needed support so he brought my mother from the Midwest to New Jersey to spend time with me and help me recover. I was so grateful for the time we had and for her insight. She had also suffered a heart attack and had endured her own open-heart surgery. She knew what I was going through, the very things I was experiencing.

Our church family was also very present and supporting during this time. Our discipleship group was ending, and we met the last few times at our home. I was seeing examples all around me of God's love and ways He shows His love through His servants in Christ.

I was happy to be home and would spend the next few weeks focusing on the new reality of life. Things would certainly be different but the important things in life were coming into focus. My desire to grow closer to God was stronger than ever before. Examples of his love and provisions were all around me.

I went back to work the first week of December. My husband drove me to work my first day back because I was still not ready to drive. The doctors had warned about the healing process with my chest wall and the need to be as far away from the airbag in the car as I could.

Well, I'm a little 'vertically challenged' at only 5'1" so driving a car meant I could not be far from the steering wheel. The length (or lack of length) of my legs meant I would have to sit close to the steering wheel to drive. I was still carrying around the "friendly pillow" I'd gotten after my surgery. This made driving difficult as well. It was just easier and safer to have my husband drive me around.

I tell you all of this because I truly did not expect my husband to hand me the keys to the car when I came out of the office the afternoon of my first day back at work. He met me at the door and asked if I could drive home. I knew something was wrong because this loving, protective man would never ask me to do something he knew I didn't want to do unless it was necessary.

My husband told me he wasn't feeling well and needed me to drive him to the urgent care clinic. I asked him to describe his symptoms. He told me he was having a lot of pain in his abdomen and had been nauseous all day. Based on what he was telling me, we decided a trip to the emergency room was much more in line with what was needed.

I turned the car around and we headed to the hospital that my husband had taken me to only five weeks earlier. He was in obvious pain and the rush hour traffic was bad that day, but we made our way as quickly and safely as possible.

We read in Isaiah 54:10 about the love God has for us. We are warned that troubles will come but we are given a promise that we can hold on to the love of God which will never fail. Isaiah tells us this promise from God,

> "'For the mountains shall depart and the hills be removed, but My kindness shall not depart from you, nor shall My covenant of peace be removed,' says the LORD, who has mercy on you."

I won't lie. I questioned God on the way to the hospital. It had only been five weeks since my heart attack. How could he let my husband get sick now? *This wasn't happening – was it?*

We arrived at the hospital that Tuesday evening and the nurses checked my husband for signs of a cardiac emergency. Thankfully, he was not having a heart attack, but he was in definite pain. They told us to have a seat in the waiting room and they would call us back as soon as a room was available.

I sent a text to our pastor and a few friends asking them to pray. Roger was alternating from sitting in the waiting room chair to hugging it while sitting on the floor. No matter what he did he could not get relief from the pain, and the wait was excruciating.

I don't blame the hospital for the wait. The waiting room was filled with patients needing help just like my husband, but it tore me up to see him in such pain.

Our pastor and a friend arrived at the hospital to wait with us. After almost a two hour wait, I asked the receptionist if I could give my husband something for the pain. She checked with the doctor and they decided to bring him back to a room. The doctor would order some tests and a few hours later we would get the diagnosis of an infected gall bladder. The tests would show that the infection had reached the point of becoming septic. My husband would need antibiotics and then surgery to remove the source of the infection.

Whew, gall bladder! No big deal! Well, leave it to my husband to do things his own way.

My husband was admitted and put on a course of antibiotics. He would be taken down for surgery to remove his gall bladder on Thursday. I had mine removed several years earlier and knew the drill. The surgery should take about an hour or so and a few days recovering then back to normal. My husband and I joked with each other and the nurses before I kissed him as they were taking him in to the operating room.

I went to the waiting area and checked the board with the names of all of the patients that showed their status. My husband's line indicated he'd been moved back to pre-op, then to the operating room, and then it updated to show the procedure was done. The surgeon came out and spoke to me telling me things had gone well and my husband was now in post-op. We should expect a few days in the hospital to take the needed antibiotics but all should be good now.

I let the family know, grabbed a bite to eat and came back to the waiting area. I waited there for a few hours expecting to receive notification my husband was being moved back to his room. I watched as the other names on the board changed status and families were called back to retrieve their loved ones. At one point, I walked to my husband's assigned hospital room thinking they must have moved him and simply forgot to tell me. *What was taking so long?*

Some family friends came to sit with me while I waited. Eventually, I asked the lady at the desk if she could check on my husband. All of the other names had disappeared from the board and I needed to know what was going on.

A few minutes later the anesthesiologist came out to talk with me. She advised me there had been some complications and my husband was not waking up or breathing on his own. He was still sedated and on a ventilator that was breathing for him.

What? This was gall bladder surgery. What complications?

Roger was moved to the intensive care unit and was kept on a ventilator that night. I have not been able to lose the vision of my husband laying in the hospital bed connected to all of those machines, especially the one that was breathing for him. My husband has always been a very strong man and rarely gets sick. It was frightening to process the thought of him not being with me and I cried out to God.

I thought I had given up my need to control but that monster came back quickly. *What could I do? What could I have done differently? Did I tell him I loved him enough?*

All of these thoughts went through my head as I listened to the ventilator breathe for him that night. I wanted him back. I wanted him back right now!

Thankfully, the truth of God's Word was hidden in my heart. I was scared and needed to know that God was in control here, too. Scripture tells us in many places where to look in times of trouble – *look to God*. We are told where our help comes from – *it comes from God*. So where should we turn?

Psalm 34:17-19 tells us to cry out to God.

> "The righteous cry out and the Lord hears, and delivers them out of all their troubles. The Lord is near to those who have a broken heart, and saves such as have a contrite spirit. Many are the afflictions of the righteous, but the Lord delivers him out of them all."

I cried out to God that night and asked that He heal my husband. I knew that God was in control and He understood the fear in my heart. It wasn't that I didn't trust God, I did. I just wanted the man I loved to be healed. God loves him more than I do, so I knew my husband was in good hands.

The hospital staff came in the next morning to try waking Roger and to remove the breathing tube. His hands were restrained because he kept trying to pull the tube out on his own every time they woke him up. His breathing was still not where they wanted it to be, so he remained on the ventilator.

At one point, they decided to wake him to a more alert state. I could talk to him and he shook his head to indicate whether or not he understood. He was still trying to get the restraints off but the nurses made certain they were tight and he wouldn't be able to get free.

It was late Friday morning when they decided to take some blood gases to determine if he was getting enough oxygen when the ventilator was turned down. They needed to make certain he was breathing well enough before taking him off the machines. Based on his reaction, he was.

The technician came in and inserted the needle to take the blood gas sample. She had some problems getting the needle in the right place and my husband showed he was in pain. She eventually gave up and went to get someone else to do the procedure. Roger indicated he wanted to write something so I handed him a pen and held up a piece of paper so he could write.

"Don't let her touch me again!" he scribbled on the paper. *He was back, fully back and aware! Hallelujah!*

It wasn't long and his breathing tube was removed. He spent the next day in ICU and was climbing the walls by the time they let him go back to the regular room. He would spend another three days in the hospital getting the needed IV antibiotics and would finally come home one week after the ordeal began.

I relearned a few very important lessons through this experience. The first was that my husband is not a very good patient. Good luck to everyone if he should end up back in the hospital. The second was that I am really not in control of what will or won't happen. The third – and most important – *was that God is in control!*

He knows all things and works them out for good. He provides all the peace and comfort we can ever need as long as we know Him and trust in Him to do so. We read in 1 Peter 5:10,

> "But may the God of all grace, who called us to His eternal glory by Christ Jesus, after you have suffered a while, perfect, establish, strengthen, and settle you."

He had to bring us to and through this suffering so we could truly know Him and trust Him.

God showed His faithfulness again, and I found peace. It came quicker this time because I knew where to look, and I looked sooner. I knew where to look because I had been there before and had learned the lessons God wanted me to learn.

Psalm 55:8 tells us where to run in times of trouble.

> "I would hasten my escape from the windy storm and tempest."

We should run, not walk, to the arms of God anytime we are faced with a storm. He is our source of shelter and true peace.

Christmas came two weeks after my husband's release from the hospital. We made a mad dash trip to Florida so he could see his mother and sister before returning for the end of year. The Year of 2012 had brought us many challenges and many changes, but the best thing that came out of that year was our focus on the one source of all things – *our faith in God*. We celebrated the beginning of the New Year and gave thanks for the gift of life.

Chapter 11

Building A Shelter From Life's Storms

*²⁴ Therefore whoever hears these sayings of Mine, and does them,
I will liken him to a wise man who built his house on the rock;
²⁵ and the rain descended, the floods came,
and the winds blew and beat on that house;
and it did not fall, for it was founded on the rock.
²⁶ But everyone who hears these sayings of
Mine, and does not do them,
will be like a foolish man who built his house on the sand;
²⁷ and the rain descended, the floods came,
and the winds blew and beat on that house;
and it fell. And great was its fall.
Matthew 7:24-27*

How many times have we heard the verses from Matthew 7 preached from the pulpit on Sunday mornings? It's easy to overlook the importance of this message. There is a lesson in the story and we are urged to reflect on where we have built our foundation. *Where have you placed your hope and faith?*

We've also heard about the importance of how seeds are planted and cultivated as described in Matthew 13. Jesus tells us that after the seeds had been planted, some were eaten by the birds because they had fallen by the wayside and never entered the soil. Others fell in stony places but withered and died because they had no depth to protect them. Some fell among thorns and were choked out. Finally, He tells us some fell on good ground and yielded a good crop but not every seed yielded the same amount. All that were planted in good soil and cared for yielded some crop and were considered good even though not all had the same result.

Where have you built your house?
How deep is your seed planted?
Is it being watered and cared for by the Word of God?

Some people have asked me why I've chosen to write this book. What makes my story so special? Well, honestly there is not much that makes my story any different than anyone else living with heart disease or challenges in life. That is, nothing other than our obedience to God's leading that brought us to Him and resulted in my decision to not worry about what life will bring my way.

I am so grateful and thankful for the wonderful church family we have found in our local church. The discipleship/Bible study group we spent so many Friday nights with came along side us and helped us learn and grow in the knowledge of our Lord and Savior. Our group went through many challenges together over the years. We ministered to each other as each crisis arose and were there to lovingly support one another through the storms. They taught us how to "*be Christians*" instead of just being church goers.

So many of us live day to day worried about what could happen. I spent years wasting opportunities for happiness because I thought I was in control or could control so much that is not mine *TO* control. If you haven't guessed it yet, control was and is my issue.

I could blame it on work hazard since I've spent many years in professions that require me to be in control to do my job. There are times where I do need to take control of certain situations and tasks, but I had abused that responsibility and turned it into a right I felt I had over my life and those around me. I could not have been more wrong.

Don't get me wrong. There are things I can control today. I need to know the boundaries and accept them.

I can control when I choose to get out of bed, *but not whether or not I wake up.*

I can control what food I put in my mouth, *but not whether or not I have an appetite.*

I can choose who I allow to be around me, *but not who I love or who will love me.*

I am not without control, but I am no longer in denial about what I can control. I am not a victim. I am survivor, and I choose to live a life full of opportunities and peace.

Where does that peace come from? How did I find it? How can someone else find it?

If you are seeking for the peace that only comes from truly knowing a loving and caring God, then you need to be actively seeking after Him. Do not be fooled in much of today's trickery that going to church is old school and you can find God on your own. God is bigger than any church but you do need people to come along side you, hold you accountable, and help you grow.

Find a church that teaches the Bible and attend regularly. Get involved in active and purposeful study of God's word. Ask someone to hold you accountable and be willing to be someone else's accountability partner. Be a disciple and a disciple maker of God's Word.

I recently attended a luncheon with several ladies from my church. The speaker at the luncheon spoke about the woman healed of the bleeding issue. The woman was seen as unclean in her day because of this ongoing problem. She had sought out many doctors and specialists in the twelve years she had been plagued with the bleeding.

No one had been able to find a solution to this woman's problem, and she had all but given up when word came that Jesus of Nazareth was coming to town. She knew she was unclean and perceived that He would not see her but she trusted that if she could only get close enough to touch His robe she would be healed. Now, that is faith.

We read about this story in Matthew Chapter 9 and Mark Chapter 5, but it is the account in Luke Chapter 8 that I will reference. Jesus immediately knew power had left Him when she touched His robe. He turned and inquired of who had touched Him but His disciples had no way of knowing who it was because of the crowd, but Jesus knew. The woman knew He did and she confessed her healing in front of all.

Jesus' response is recorded in Luke 8:48,

> "And He said to her, 'Daughter, be of good cheer, your faith has made you well. Go in peace.'"

I haven't physically touched Jesus' robe but I have felt His love and healing in my life. The Bible doesn't tell us this woman never had another health issue, but it does say she was healed from her current affliction and that healing happened immediately. I can trust that if only the touching of Jesus' robe could heal this woman, then I can be healed by His Word and my faith in it.

What happens if my health doesn't remain on a 'good' track? What if I get sick again? Well, the Bible has an answer for that as well.

Paul writes about how he responded to God refusing to remove his infirmity. He tells us in 2 Corinthians 12:8 that he pleaded with God three times to remove that which plagued him, but God didn't remove it. In fact, Paul continues in 2 Corinthians 12:9[a] that God responded,

> "My grace is sufficient for you, for My strength is made perfect in weakness."

Paul goes on to tell us that he would boast in his infirmities so the power of Christ would rest upon him. I want that power, too.

Paul doesn't stop there, though. He continues in verse 10,

> "Therefore I take pleasure in infirmities, in reproaches, in needs, in persecutions, in distresses, for Christ's sake. For when I am weak, then I am strong."

Wow! We get power when we are down and let God work in our lives. It is no longer about our strength but rather it is about God's strength. He was strong enough to hang the stars and spin our planet in to orbit. He is certainly strong enough to handle this little, temporary challenge I have before me today.

So, back to the question of why I wrote this book and what makes me special. God makes me special and God can heal. God gives peace and my hope is that sharing the peace I've found will help others search out the true source of that peace.

Why did Jesus call out the woman who had touched his robe? He could have simply continued to walk on but He didn't. Did He want to scold her? No, He wanted people to know He had healed her and that is why I feel compelled to share our story.

I wish I could say everything was better the next year. It was but not in the way most people would define better. My husband stayed healthy and he was able to find a new job with a salary better than the one he had lost the year before. I was still at my new job but my health continued to present challenges. By the end of the year, I had eight stents to go with my four cardiac by-passes. One of the by-passes had failed and so did the stent that was placed to try to open the artery again. I was living with one fully blocked artery, *but I was living*.

The following year brought better health but changes at work. We continued to be faithful in our study of the Word to grow closer to God. Our pastor asked us to share our testimony with the church and we scheduled our 'talk' for the first weekend in February.

My boss sent me an email the Friday before and asked to meet with me on Sunday afternoon. For the record, it is rarely a good thing when your boss flies across the ocean and asks to meet with you on a Sunday evening. It wasn't this time either.

I was given news that our company would be closing and I had to lay everyone off the next day. I knew something big was coming when he sent the email, but we were still able to talk about God's love and provision of peace that Sunday morning even though the unknown lingered just hours away.

We read in Philippians 4:19,

> "And my God shall supply all your need according to His riches in glory by Christ Jesus."

I am not worried about what will happen with my job. My husband and I are trying to be better stewards with our finances and responsible with the blessings God has given us. We do not hope for troubles, but we know that God will see us through whatever may come, as long as we keep our eyes focused on Him and are willing to follow His leading.

Speaking of following His leading, what example did Jesus give us while He was here on Earth? He taught us to serve. Mark 10:45 tells us,

> "For even the Son of Man did not come to be served, but to serve, and to give His life a ransom for many."

God calls us to serve Him and others. We are not saved so we can sit in a church pew for an hour or two on a Sunday morning. We are called to be out in the world, serving the needy and sharing

God's love with all. We are called to minister to others for God's glory, not our own.

What on earth is there to worry about tomorrow when we cannot change what is not here yet? We must choose to take care of today and trust that God is in control of tomorrow. *Serve where you can, when you can.* God will use your efforts and bless those who are obedient.

There are many verses in the Bible that give me strength and courage. Isaiah is filled with so many of them I am tempted to copy and paste the whole book here and let you pick out your favorites. Common sense tells me that would not be prudent so I am going to share one that gives me hope in life's storms. Isaiah 25:4 tells us,

> "For You have been a strength to the poor; a strength to the needy in his distress, a refuge from the storm, a shade from the heat; for the blast of the terrible ones is a storm against the wall."

Who is a strength for the poor? God is.
Who is a strength for the needy in his distress? God is.
Who is a refuge from the storm? God is.
Who is a shade from the heat? God is.

I am not able to control what is going to happen, but I can choose how I approach life. I can be disappointed by the challenges or I can choose to live despite them. I choose to live and be thankful for the life God gives me. I choose to use the storms of my life to help others find the hope only God can give. There is no promise of tomorrow, but there is the promise from God that He will give me what I need for whatever tomorrow may bring.

God has blessed our family with today. We are trying to give back a little of what He has given us. He has called us to serve Him and share His Word. The blessings we are getting from being obedient to Him cannot be measured. One of the biggest is the opportunity to take our eyes off ourselves and see others through

God's eyes. We find it hard to pity ourselves when we are serving others.

Jesus called Peter to serve Him after testing and refining his faith. Peter had walked on water with Jesus but still denied Him three times while Jesus was being brought to trial. Jesus gave Peter three chances for redemption in John 21:15-17.

> "So when they had eaten breakfast, Jesus said to Simon Peter, 'Simon, *son* of Jonah, do you love Me more than these?' He said to Him, 'Yes, Lord; You know that I love You.' He said to him, 'Feed My lambs.'
>
> He said to him again a second time, 'Simon, *son* of Jonah, do you love Me?' He said to Him, 'Yes, Lord; You know that I love You.' He said to him, 'Tend My sheep.'
>
> He said to him the third time, 'Simon, *son* of Jonah, do you love Me?' Peter was grieved because He said to him the third time, 'Do you love Me?' And he said to Him, 'Lord, You know all things; You know that I love You.' Jesus said to him, 'Feed My sheep.'"

Jesus came to live among men and to die for all of our sins. He came to teach us how to live for God and not ourselves. He came to show love, the love of God. If you are reading this right now, know that God loves you enough to have sent His son to die for *YOU*. There is nothing you are going through He does not understand and cannot control. Trust Him and He will guide you always.

God has called all of us to serve Him and spread His Word. There is more peace than you can imagine when you surrender to God's will and seek to serve Him. We continue to have struggles in life, but we are blessed through them and because we have chosen to serve God. There are many ways to serve Him, and not all are called to serve the same way. Find the way God wants to use you and surrender to that calling. You will be blessed.

We are called to learn, grow, and then disciple. He loves you and calls those that love Him to serve Him. We pray that you will be obedient to the calling God has placed on your life and that you will have opportunities to serve God and reap the rewards of the true peace and happiness that can only come from the One that loves us.

REFERENCES

All scripture taken from the New King James Version®. Copyright © 1982 by Thomas Nelson, Inc. Used by permission. All rights reserved.

Printed in the United States
By Bookmasters